WORDS FROM THE BIBLE ABOUT GRATITUDE

Be Grateful

Edited and designed by Ben Alex

scandinavia

BE GRATEFUL
WORDS FROM THE BIBLE ABOUT GRATITUDE

Published by Scandinavia Publishing House 2012
Scandinavia Publishing House
Drejervej 15,3, DK-2400 Copenhagen, NV
Denmark
E-mail: info@scanpublishing.dk
Web: www.scanpublishing.dk

Concept, editing and design by Ben Alex
All quotes from New International Version unless otherwise noted
Photo copyright © Dreamstime pages 2,18,32,50,60,70,82,84,96,99,104,109,122
Photo copyright © Janis Zroback pages 8,10,15,23,24,28,35,36,41,42,49,57,58,62,69,75,81,87,93,94,102,110,115,116,119,127
Visit Janis at http://www.redbubble.com/people/paintability

Printed in China
ISBN 978 87 7132 046 6
All rights reserved

Let the word of Christ
dwell in you richly as you teach
and admonish one another with
all wisdom, and as you sing psalms, hymns
and spiritual songs with gratitude
in your hearts to God.

Colossians 3:16

Speak to one another
with psalms, hymns and spiritual songs.
Sing and make music in your
heart to the Lord.

Ephesians 5:19

> Give thanks to the LORD,
> for he is good; his love
> endures forever.
>
> 1 Chronicles 16:34

> Therefore I will praise you,
> O Lord, among the nations;
> I will sing praises to your name.
>
> 2 Samuel 22:50

Is any one of you in trouble?
He should pray. Is anyone happy?
Let him sing songs of praise.

James 5:13

Oh give thanks to Yahweh.
Call on his name. Make his doings known
among the peoples.

1 Chronicles 16:8 WEB

I will give you thanks
in the great assembly;
among throngs of people
I will praise you.

Psalm 35:18

Now, our God,
we give you thanks,
and praise your
glorious name.

1 Chronicles 29:13

Dream Big Girl

You have filled my heart
with greater joy than when their grain
and new wine abound.

Psalm 4:7

I will give thanks to the Lord
because of his righteousness and will sing praise
to the name of the Lord Most High.

Psalm 7:17

I thank and praise you,
God of my ancestors,
for you have given me
wisdom and strength.

Daniel 2:23

The Lord is my strength and shield.
I trust him with all my heart. He helps me,
and my heart is filled with joy.
I burst out in songs of thanksgiving.

Psalm 28:7

He prayed three times a day,
just as he had always done,
giving thanks to his God.

Daniel 6:10

I will praise you forever
for what you have done;
in your name I will hope,
for your name is good.

Psalm 52:9

My heart is steadfast,
O God, my heart is steadfast;
I will sing and make music.

Psalm 57:7

...that my heart may sing
to you and not be silent.
O Lord my God, I will give
you thanks forever.

Psalm 30:12

Awake, my soul!
Awake, harp and lyre!
I will awaken the dawn.

Psalm 57:8

Do not be anxious
about anything, but in everything,
by prayer and petition, with thanksgiving,
present your requests to God.

Philippians 4:6

So they rolled the stone aside.
Then Jesus looked up to heaven
and said, "Father, thank you
for hearing me."

John 11:41 NLT

On that same occasion
Jesus was filled by the Holy Spirit
with rapturous joy. "I give Thee fervent thanks,"
He exclaimed, "O Father, Lord of Heaven and earth,
that Thou hast hidden these things from sages
and men of understanding, and hast revealed
them to babes. Yes, Father, for such
has been Thy gracious will.

Luke 10:21 WNT

hankful heart

At that very moment
she came up and began giving thanks
to God, and continued to speak of Him
to all those who were looking for
the redemption of Jerusalem.

Luke 2:38 NASB

Peter said to Jesus,
"Rabbi, we are thankful to you
that we are here. Let us put up three tents —
one for you, one for Moses,
and one for Elijah."

Mark 9:5 WNT

After he said this,
he took some bread and gave
thanks to God in front of them all.
Then he broke it and began to eat.

Acts 27:35

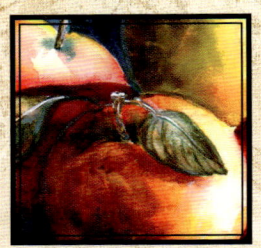

Then Jesus took the loaves,
gave thanks to God, and
distributed them to the people.
Afterward he did the same with the fish.
And they all ate as much as they wanted.

John 6:11

For everything
God created is good,
and nothing is to be rejected
if it is received with
thanksgiving.

1 Timothy 4:4

Then some boats from Tiberias
landed near the place where the people had
eaten the bread after the Lord
had given thanks.

John 6:23

> Save us,
> O God of our salvation.
> And gather us and deliver us
> from the nations to give thanks
> to Your holy name and
> glory in Your praise
>
> 1 Chronicles 16:35 NASB

But I trust in
your unfailing love.
I will rejoice because you
have rescued me.

Psalm 13:5 NLT

The gift of

He fell to the ground
at Jesus' feet, thanking him for
what he had done.

Luke 17:16 NLT

I always thank my God for you
and for the gracious gifts he has given you,
now that you belong to Christ Jesus.

1 Corinthians 1:4 ESV

Let them
give thanks to the Lord
for His lovingkindness and
for His wonders to the
sons of men!

Psalm 107:15

Let your roots
grow down into him,
and let your lives be built on him.
Then your faith will grow strong in
the truth you were taught, and you
will overflow with thankfulness.

Colossians 2:7 NLT

In everything give thanks;
for this is God's will for you
in Christ Jesus.

1 Thessalonians 5:18 NASB

Devote yourselves
to prayer, being watchful
and thankful.

Colossians 4:2

I give thanks to my God...

1 Corinthians 14:18a YLT

Shout for joy,
O heavens; rejoice, O earth;
burst into song, O mountains!
For the LORD comforts his people
and will have compassion
on his afflicted ones.

Isaiah 49:13

Heartfelt thanks be to
the God and Father of our Lord Jesus Christ –
the Father who is full of compassion and
the God who gives all comfort.

2 Corinthians 1:3 WNT

But to God be the thanks
who in Christ ever heads our triumphal procession,
and by our hands waves in every place that
sweet incense, the knowledge of Him.

2 Corinthians 2:14 WNT

Therefore, since we are receiving
a kingdom that cannot be shaken,
let us be thankful, and so worship God
acceptably with reverence and awe...

Hebrews 12:28

That I may tell of all Your praises;
that in the gates of the daughter of Zion
I may rejoice in Your salvation.

Psalm 9:14 NASB

I urge, then, first of all,
that requests, prayers,
intercession and thanksgiving
be made for everyone.

1 Timothy 2:1

First, I thank my God
through Jesus Christ for all of you,
because your faith is being
reported all over the world.

Romans 1:8

And they said,
"We give thanks to you,
Lord God, the Almighty, the one
who is and who always was, for now you have
assumed your great power and
have begun to reign."

Revelation 11:17 NLT

Thankfulness

It is good to
give thanks to the Lord,
to sing praises to
the Most High.

Psalm 92:1 NLT

With praise and thanksgiving
they sang to the Lord: "He is good;
his love to Israel endures forever."

Ezra 3:11

...the sounds of joy and gladness,
the voices of bride and bridegroom,
and the voices of those who bring thank offerings
to the house of the Lord, saying, "Give thanks
to the Lord Almighty, for the Lord is good;
his love endures forever."

Jeremiah 33:11

Praise ye the LORD.
O give thanks unto the Lord;
for he is good: for his mercy
endureth for ever.

Psalm 106:1 ERV

When all the Israelites saw
the fire coming down and the glory
of the Lord above the temple, they knelt
on the pavement with their faces to the ground,
and they worshiped and gave thanks to
the Lord, saying, "He is good;
his love endures forever."

2 Chronicles 7:3

We thank you, O God!
We give thanks because
you are near.

Psalm 75:1

With my mouth
I will give thanks abundantly
to the Lord; and in the midst
of many I will praise Him.

Psalm 109:30

Give thanks
to the Lord,
for he is good!
His faithful love
endures forever.

Psalm 118:1 NLT

Then Hannah prayed and said:
"My heart rejoices in the Lord; in the Lord
my horn is lifted high."

1 Samuel 2:1a

...the living creatures give glory,
honor and thanks to him who sits on the throne
and who lives for ever and ever...

Revelation 4:9

And David danced
before the Lord with
all his might.

2 Samuel 6:14 ESV

Sing to him,
sing praise to him;
tell of all his wonderful acts.

1 Chronicles 16:9

Sing praises to the LORD
who reigns in Jerusalem. Tell the world about
his unforgettable deeds.

Psalm 9:11

nd honor

My soul will be satisfied as with the richest of foods;
with singing lips my mouth will praise you.

Psalm 63:5

Praise the Lord with the harp;
make music to him on the ten-stringed lyre.

Psalm 33:2

Sing praises to the Lord,
O you his saints, and give thanks
to his holy name.

Psalm 30:4

Sing praises to God,
sing praises; sing praises to our King,
sing praises.

Psalm 47:6

Let them praise
his name in the dance:
let them sing praises to him with
the tambourine and harp.

Psalm 149:3

The officers and the trumpeters
were beside the king, and all the people
of the land were rejoicing and blowing trumpets,
and singers with musical instruments
were leading the praises.

2 Chronicles 23:13

Praise him with the tambourine and dancing;
praise him with the strings and flute.

Psalm 150:4

My tongue will speak
of your righteousness and of
your praises all day long.

Psalm 35:28

Who is like You,
O LORD?
Who is like You,
majestic in holiness,
Awesome in praises,
working wonders?

Exodus 15:11 NASB

And again,
"Praise the Lord,
all you Gentiles,
and sing praises to him,
all you peoples."

Romans 15:11

About midnight Paul and Silas
were praying and singing hymns to God,
and the other prisoners were
listening to them.

Acts 16:25

But when the multitudes saw it,
they marveled and glorified God,
who had given such authority to men.

Matthew 9:8

You will also thank the Father,
who has made you able to share the light,
which is what God's people inherit.

Colossians 1:12 GWT

...always giving thanks
to God the Father for everything,
in the name of our Lord
Jesus Christ.

Ephesians 5:20

He says, "I will declare your name
to my brothers; in the presence of the congregation
I will sing your praises."

Hebrews 2:12

They have comforted me,
and they have comforted you.
Therefore, show people like these
your appreciation.

1 Corinthians 16:18 GWT

I thank my God always,
making mention of you in my prayers.

Philemon 1:4 NASB

We always thank God for all of you
and pray for you constantly.

1 Thessalonians 1:2 NLT

Receive him therefore
in the Lord with all gladness.
Give him a glad welcome.

Philippians 2:29 PNT

Timothy, I thank God for you...

2 Timothy 1:3 NLT

I always thank my God for you
and for the gracious gifts he has given you,
now that you belong to Christ Jesus.

1 Corinthians 1:4 NLT

Dear brothers and sisters,
we can't help but thank God for you,
because your faith is flourishing and your
love for one another is growing.

2 Thessalonians 1:3 NLT

As for us, we can't
help but thank God for you,
dear brothers and sisters loved by the Lord.
We are always thankful that God
chose you to be among the first
to experience salvation.

2 Thessalonians 2:13a NLT

My heart is
confident, O God.
My heart is confident.
I want to sing and
make music.

Psalm 57:7 GWT

They risked
their lives for me.
Not only I but all the churches
of the Gentiles are grateful
to them.

Romans 16:4

Sing to the LORD
with grateful praise;
make music to our God on the harp.
He covers the sky with clouds;
he supplies the earth with rain
and makes grass grow on the hills.

Psalm 147:7-8

For God is the
King of all the earth.
Sing praises with
understanding.

Psalm 47:7 WEB

Be anxious for nothing,
but in everything by prayer and supplication,
with thanksgiving, let your requests
be made known to God.

Philippians 4:6 NKJV

O my Strength,
I sing praise to you;
you, O God, are my fortress,
my loving God.

Psalm 59:17

I will praise God's name
in song and glorify him
with thanksgiving.

Psalm 69:30

I will thank you,
Lord, among all the people.
I will sing your praises
among the nations.

Psalm 57:9 NLT

That I may proclaim
with the voice of thanksgiving
and declare all Your wonders.

Psalm 26:7

And since it is through God's kindness,
then it is not by their good works. For in that case,
God's grace would not be what it really is –
free and undeserved.

Romans 11:6 NLT

For by grace you
have been saved through faith.
And this is not your own doing;
it is the gift of God...

Ephesians 2:8 ESV

nd grace

Grace and peace to you
from God our Father and
the Lord Jesus Christ.

1 Corinthians 1:3

Being justified freely
by his grace, through the redemption,
that is in Christ Jesus...

Romans 3:24 DRB

We believe that
we are all saved the same way,
by the undeserved grace
of the Lord Jesus.

Acts 15:11 NLT

...made us alive with Christ
even when we were dead in transgressions –
it is by grace you have been saved.

Ephesians 2:5

But we have
something to celebrate,
something to be happy about.
This brother of yours
was dead but has
come back to life.
He was lost but
has been found.

Luke 15:32 GWT

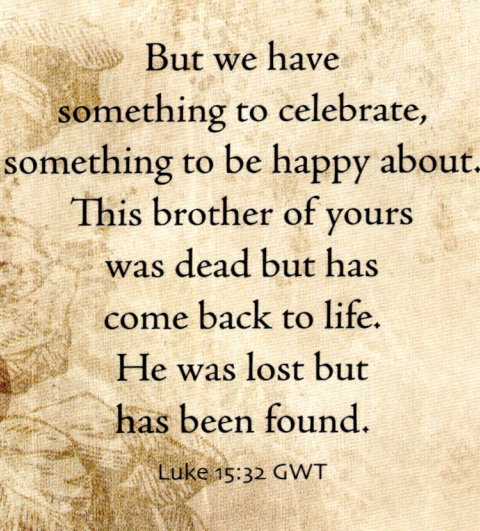

...it is certainly true that God's kindness and the gift given through the kindness of one person, Jesus Christ, have been showered on humanity.

Romans 5:15 GWT

Every good and perfect gift is from above,
coming down from the father of heavenly lights,
who does not change like shifting sand.

James 1:17

Bring the fattened calf and kill it.
Let's have a feast and celebrate.

Luke 15:23

For we have great thankfulness
and encouragement through thy love…

Philemon 1:7 DBT

Praise the LORD!
I will thank the LORD with all my heart
as I meet with his godly people.

Psalm 111:1

But you are a chosen people,
a royal priesthood, a holy nation,
a people belonging to God, that you may
declare the praises of him who called you
out of darkness into his wonderful light.

1 Peter 2:9

But God created those foods
to be eaten with thanks
by faithful people who
know the truth.

1 Timothy 4:3 NLT

Then he took him in his arms
and gave praise to God...

Luke 2:28

I thank you for
answering my prayer
and giving me victory!

Psalm 118:21

Reasons to

The Lord himself
goes before you
and will be with you;
he will never leave you
nor forsake you.

Deuteronomy 31:8

be grateful

> Thanks be to God,
> who delivers me through
> Jesus Christ our Lord!
>
> Romans 7:25

I thank Christ Jesus our Lord,
who has given me strength
to do his work.
He considered me trustworthy
and appointed me to serve him,

1 Timothy 1:12

This is the day
that the Lord has made;
let us rejoice and
be glad in it.

Psalm 118:24

Give thanks
to the Lord,
for he is good,
for his steadfast love
endures forever.

Psalm 136:1

I will give thanks
to you, LORD,
with all my heart;
I will tell of all your
wonderful deeds.

Psalm 9:1a

But thanks
be to God that,
though you used to
be slaves to sin,
you have come to obey
from your heart
the pattern of teaching
that has now claimed
your allegiance.

Romans 6:17

For God so loved the world
that he gave his one and only Son,
that whoever believes in him shall not perish
but have eternal life. For God did not send his Son
into the world to condemn the world,
but to save the world
through him.

John 3:16-17

Amen! Praise and glory
and wisdom and thanks
and honor and power
and strength be to our God
for ever and ever. Amen!

Revelation 7:12

Let us come
into his presence
with thanksgiving;
let us make a joyful noise
to him with songs
of praise!

Psalm 95:2 ESV

Is not the cup of thanksgiving
for which we give thanks
a participation in the blood of Christ?
And is not the bread that we break
a participation in the body of Christ?

1 Corinthians 10:16

Give thanks to the Lord,
call on his name;
make known among the nations
what he has done, and proclaim
that his name is exalted.

Isaiah 12:4

I will sing
of your strength,
in the morning I will
sing of your love;
for you are my fortress,
my refuge in times
of trouble.

Psalm 59:16

I praise you
because I am fearfully
and wonderfully made;
your works are wonderful,
I know that full well.

Psalm 139:14

Shout for joy
to the Lord, all the earth.
Worship the Lord with gladness;
come before him with joyful songs.
Know that the Lord is God.
It is he who made us, and we are his;
we are his people, the sheep of his pasture.
Enter his gates with thanksgiving
and his courts with praise;
give thanks to him and
praise his name.

Psalm 100:1-4

Let the peace of Christ
rule in your hearts,
since as members of one body
you were called to peace.
And be thankful.

Colossians 3:15

And whatever you do,
whether in word or deed,
do it all in the name
of the Lord Jesus,
giving thanks to God
the Father through him.

Colossians 3:17

Make thankfulness
your sacrifice to God.

Psalm 50:14 NLT

The sacrifice

He who offers
a sacrifice of thanksgiving
honors Me.

Psalm 50:23

But I, with
shouts of grateful praise,
will sacrifice to you.
What I have vowed I will make good.
I will say, 'Salvation comes
from the LORD.'

Jonah 2:9

Through Jesus, therefore,
let us continually offer to God
a sacrifice of praise—
the fruit of lips that openly
profess his name.

Hebrews 13:15

Then my head will be exalted above the enemies who surround me; at his tabernacle will I sacrifice with shouts of joy; I will sing and make music to the Lord.

Psalm 27:6

We know
that in all things,
God works for the good
of those who love him.

Romans 8:28

Yes, you will be enriched
in every way so that
you can always be generous.
And when we take your gifts
to those who need them,
they will thank God.
So two good things will result
from this ministry of giving—
the needs of the believers
in Jerusalem will be met,
and they will joyfully express
their thanks to God.

2 Corinthians 9:11-12